Intermediate Technic 2

by James and Jane Smisor Bastien

KJOS WEST · Neil A. Kjos, Jr., Publisher · San Diego, California

PREFACE

The INTERMEDIATE PIANO COURSE is designed to be used after the student has completed Level 4 of the BASTIEN PIANO LIBRARY. In addition, the INTERMEDIATE PIANO COURSE may be used by a student who has completed *any* elementary piano course. This course is a comprehensive, organized program of study consisting of four books per level which may be used simultaneously for best results. The INTERMEDIATE PIANO COURSE is available in grade levels 1, 2, 3, in each of the following books.

- INTERMEDIATE REPERTOIRE
- INTERMEDIATE THEORY
- INTERMEDIATE TECHNIC
- INTERMEDIATE MULTI-KEY SOLOS

INTERMEDIATE REPERTOIRE introduces the student to many factors of each style period: Baroque, Classical, Romantic, and Contemporary. For each period there are descriptions of overall styles (dress, art, architecture), keyboard instruments, various compositions representative of each period, and a list of composers. The music is a combination of master composer works and pieces written by the Bastiens in each style period. Special emphasis is given to providing more accessible pieces in the Romantic style. The teacher may assign pieces from different periods of the Repertoire book at the same time.

INTERMEDIATE THEORY contains written and playing material to coordinate with the Repertoire book.

INTERMEDIATE TECHNIC contains exercises and etudes by the standard composers as well as many new studies by the Bastiens.

INTERMEDIATE MULTI-KEY SOLOS provides a variety of original music by the Bastiens to encourage the student to explore many keys rather than staying in the limited key selection found in master composer works at the intermediate level.

The INTERMEDIATE PIANO COURSE includes the following books:

Intermediate Repertoire 1 (WP105)	**Intermediate Technic 1** (WP111)
Intermediate Repertoire 2 (WP106)	**Intermediate Technic 2** (WP112)
Intermediate Repertoire 3 (WP107)	**Intermediate Technic 3** (WP113)
Intermediate Theory 1 (WP108)	**Intermediate Multi-key Solos 1** (WP114)
Intermediate Theory 2 (WP109)	**Intermediate Multi-key Solos 2** (WP115)
Intermediate Theory 3 (WP110)	**Intermediate Multi-key Solos 3** (WP116)

On the cover is one of many sea anemones (a sedentary marine animal with a columnar body and circles of tentacles surrounding the mouth) found in the Pacific Ocean.

CONTENTS

The Wind Machine . . . . Cornelius Gurlitt 4
Etude in G . . . . Carl Czerny 5
Alberti Bass 6
Springtime . . . . Jean B. Duvernoy 7
Phrasing 8
The Juggler . . . . Joseph Concone 9
Rotation Technic 10
Morning Ride . . . . Carl Czerny 11
Broken Chords 12
Restless Clouds . . . . James Bastien 13
The Winding River . . . . Carl Czerny 14
Repeated Notes 16
Raindrops . . . . James Bastien 17
The Singing Brook . . . . Jean B. Duvernoy 18
Song of the Cello . . . . Jane Smisor Bastien 19
The Prancing Horse . . . . Cornelius Gurlitt 20
Wrist Staccato 22
Hopscotch . . . . Jean B. Duvernoy 23
Etude in C . . . . Hermann Berens 24
Hang Gliders . . . . Louis Köhler 25
Trills 26
Song Birds . . . . Carl Czerny 27
Saturday Night Polka . . . . Louis Streabbog 28
Storm at Sea . . . . Jane Smisor Bastien 29
Etude in F . . . . Carl Czerny 30
The Noisy Woodpecker . . . . Joseph Concone 31
Part Playing 32
On the Seashore . . . . Jean B. Duvernoy 33
Double Notes 34
The Ferris Wheel . . . . Jane Smisor Bastien 35
Daydreams . . . . Jean B. Duvernoy 36
The Chase . . . . Herman Berens 37
Scales and Chords 38

Lift the right hand at each phrase ending.

The Wind Machine

Scale and phrasing study

CORNELIUS GURLITT

Etude in G
Scale study

CARL CZERNY

Chord Reference

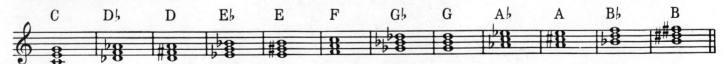

Alberti Bass

Practice these Alberti bass exercises using forearm rotation.
Rotate (turn) the forearm in the direction the notes move:

Transpose to other keys (refer to the Chord Reference above).

Say: "bottom   top middle   top"

Springtime
Alberti bass study

JEAN BAPTISTE DUVERNOY

Phrasing technic on the piano requires a change in wrist position from low to high.

Phrasing

Practice these phrasing exercises with changing wrist positions. While playing, say "down-up" for the changes in wrist position.

1.

2.

Play the exercise above using these rhythms.

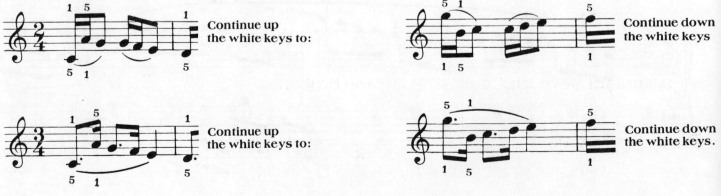

The Juggler
Phrasing study

JOSEPH CONCONE

Rotate (turn) the forearm in the direction the notes move:

Rotation Technic

Practice these rotation exercises using the correct forearm motion. Play in three tempos: slow, medium, fast.

Transpose this exercise to other keys.

Continue this pattern up the white keys.

Play the exercise above using these rhythms.

Morning Ride

Rotation study

CARL CZERNY

Broken Chords

Practice these broken chords and observe the fingerings. Memorize the fingerings for these chords. Learn one or more each week.

C Major   R.H.   1 2 3 5   1 2 ④ 5   1 2 ④ 5   Also play in F and G major. The fingering is the same.
           L.H.   5 ④ 2 1   5 ④ 2 1   5 3 2 1

D Major   R.H.   1 2 3 5   1 2 ④ 5   1 2 ④ 5   Also play in A and E major. The fingering is the same.
           L.H.   5 3 2 1   5 ④ 2 1   5 3 2 1

D♭ Major   R.H.   1 2 3 5   1 2 ④ 5   1 2 ④ 5   Also play in A♭ and E♭ major. The fingering is the same.
           L.H.   5 ④ 2 1   5 ④ 2 1   5 3 2 1

B♭ Major   R.H.   1 2 3 5   1 2 ④ 5   1 2 ④ 5   Also play in B major. The fingering is the same.
           L.H.   5 3 2 1   5 ④ 2 3   5 3 2 1

G♭ Major   R.H.   1 2 3 5   1 2 ④ 5   1 2 ④ 5
           L.H.   5 3 2 1   5 ④ 2 1   5 3 2 1
                     (4)

Restless Clouds

Broken chord study

Con spirito

JAMES BASTIEN

The Winding River

Broken chord study

CARL CZERNY

Repeated Notes

Play these repeated notes with a staccato touch (rapid finger changes combined with a bouncing wrist).

1.

Play the exercise above using a sixteenth-note pattern.

2.

Continue up the chromatic scale to C.

Continue down the chromatic scale to C.

Play the exercise above using a sixteenth-note pattern.

etc.

3.

Continue up and down the C scale.

Continue up and down the C scale.

Raindrops

Repeated note study

JAMES BASTIEN

The Singing Brook

Rotation study

Moderato

JEAN BAPTISTE DUVERNOY

Song of the Cello

Broken chord and rotation study

JANE SMISOR BASTIEN

The Prancing Horse

Repeated note study

CORNELIUS GURLITT

Wrist Staccato

When practicing these wrist staccato exercises, move both your arm and wrist up and down with a quick, light motion. Keep your fingers curved, in position for the next notes.

Practice the exercise above in the following rhythms.

Even two's

Even three's

Even four's

Dotted

Long, short-short

Short-short, long

The same exercise and rhythms may be played in octaves.

Hopscotch

Wrist Staccato study

JEAN BAPTISTE DUVERNOY

Etude in C
Velocity study

HERMANN BERENS

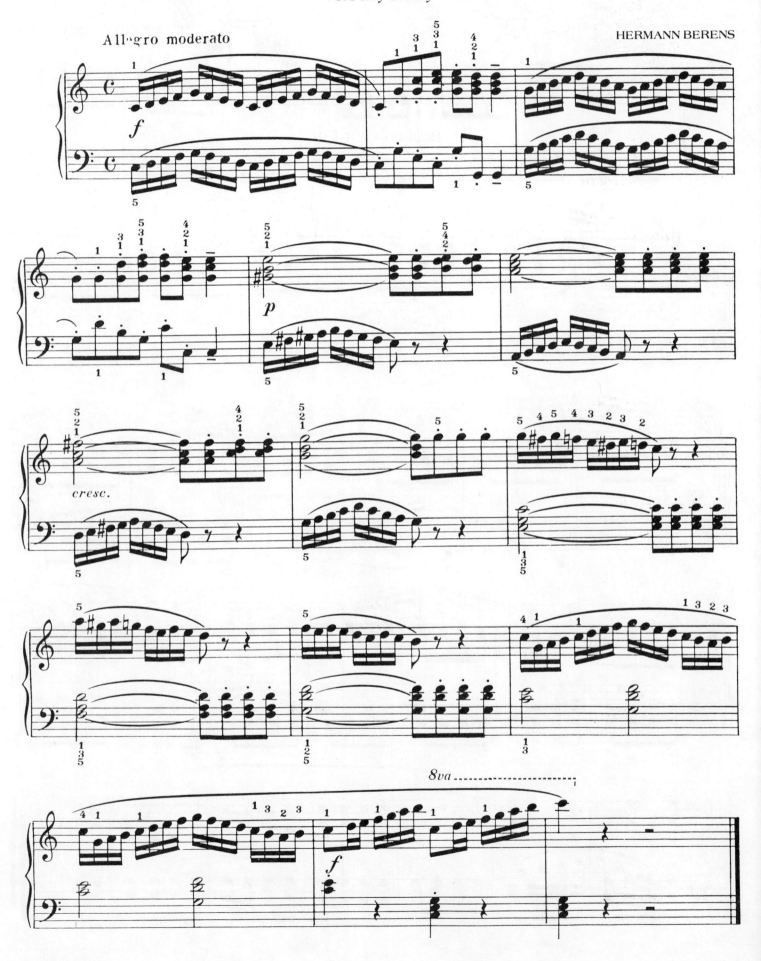

Hang Gliders

Broken chord study

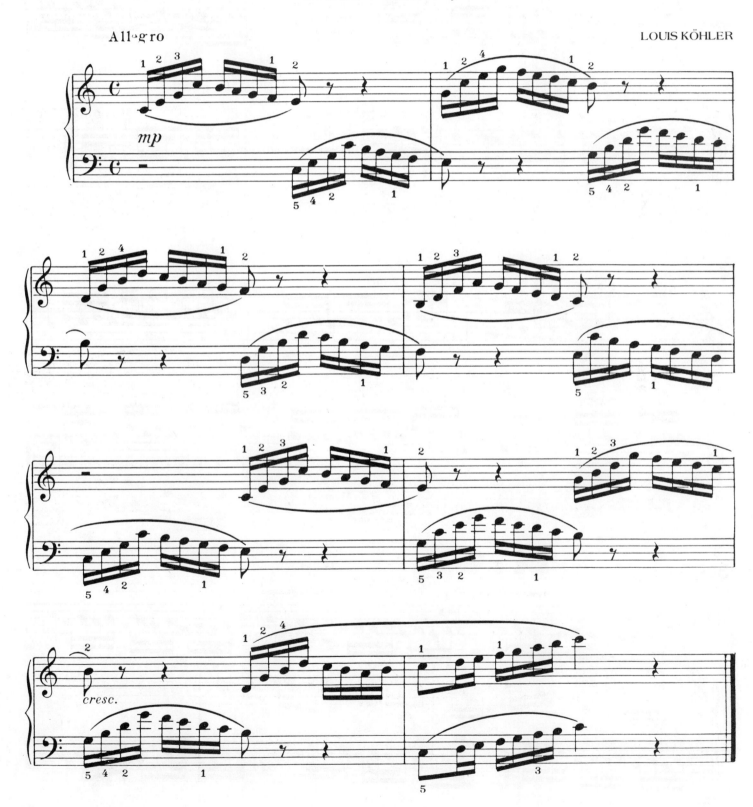

Trills

Practice these trills with strong fingers to produce an even, clear sound. Practice in different rhythms:

1.

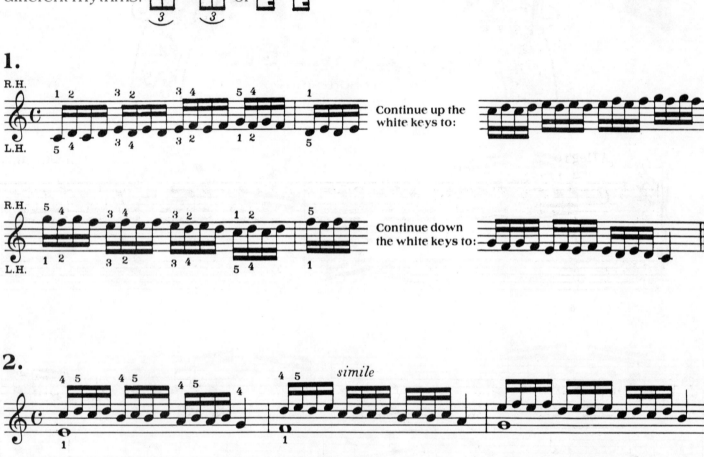

Continue up the white keys to:

Continue down the white keys to:

2.

simile

3.

simile

Song Birds

Trill study

CARL CZERNY

Allegro

Saturday Night Polka

Wrist staccato study

Allegretto

LOUIS STREABBOG

Storm at Sea

Scale study

Con spirito

JANE SMISOR BASTIEN

Etude in F

Trill study

CARL CZERNY

The Noisy Woodpecker

Wrist staccato study

JOSEPH CONCONE

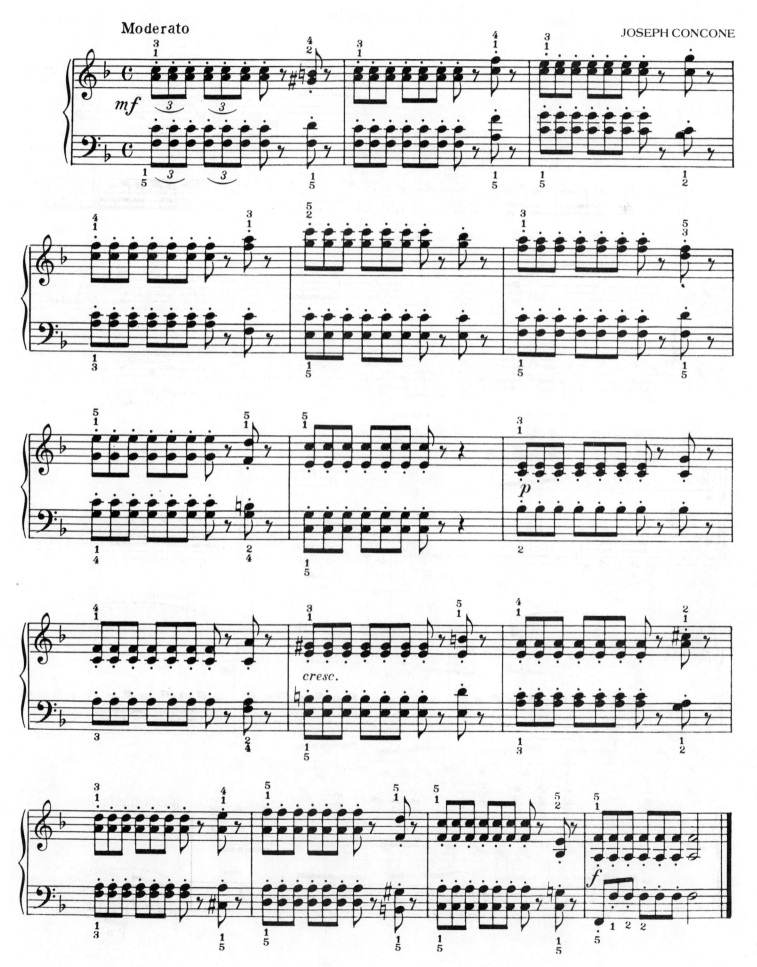

Part Playing

Practice these exercises holding the tied notes while playing the moving notes. Play either hands separately or together.

1.

Continue this pattern up the white keys.

2.

Continue this pattern up the white keys.

3.

Hold down fingers 2-4 throughout.

Continue this pattern up the white keys.

4.

Continue this pattern up the white keys.

On the Seashore

Part playing

Allegretto

JEAN BAPTISTE DUVERNOY

Double Notes

Play these double note exercises with a legato touch. Play either hands separately or together.

1.

legato

Continue this pattern up the keyboard on the white keys.

Play the exercise above using these rhythms.

etc.

etc.

2.

The Ferris Wheel
Double notes study

Parallel thirds study

Allegretto

JANE SMISOR BASTIEN

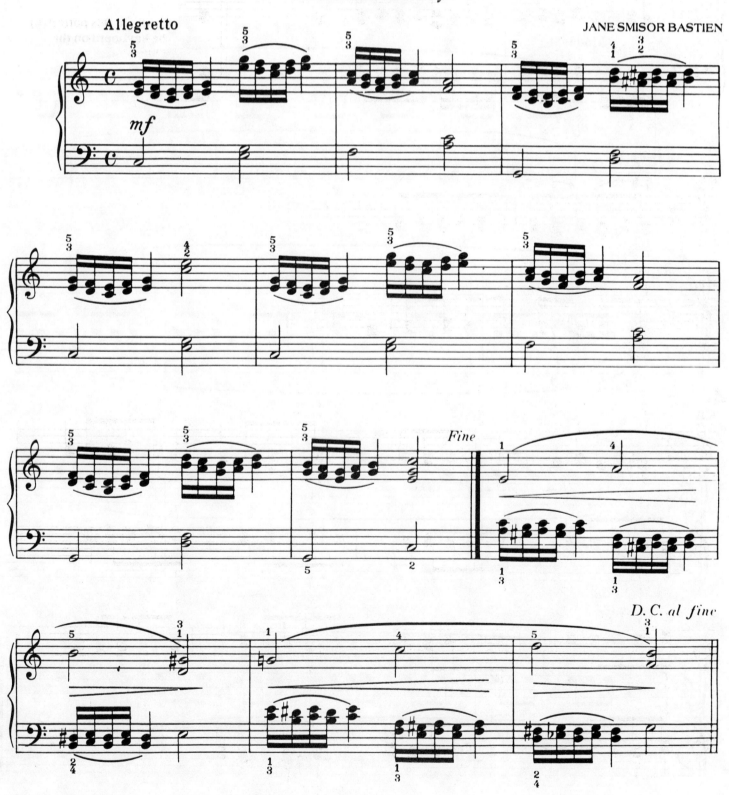

Play the half notes very legato and the repeated notes staccato.

Daydreams

Part playing

Moderato

JEAN BAPTISTE DUVERNOY

The Chase

Chromatic scale study

HERMAN BERENS

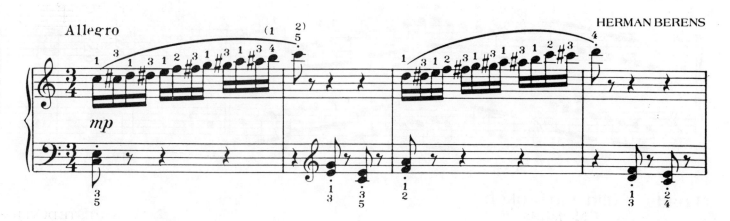

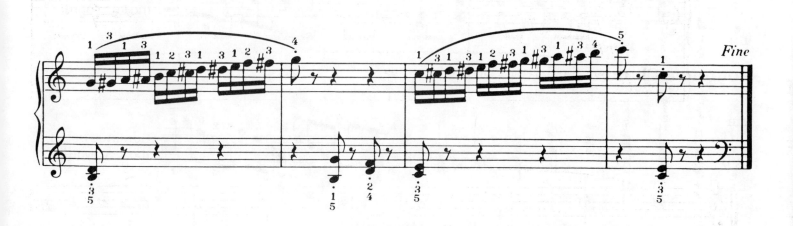

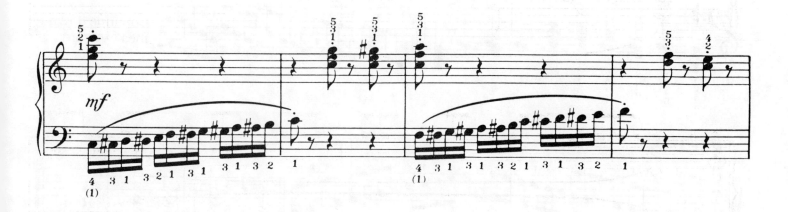

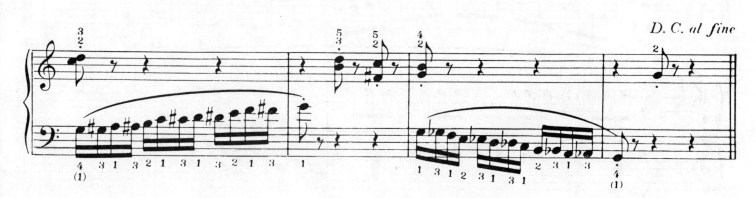

Scales and Chords

C Major

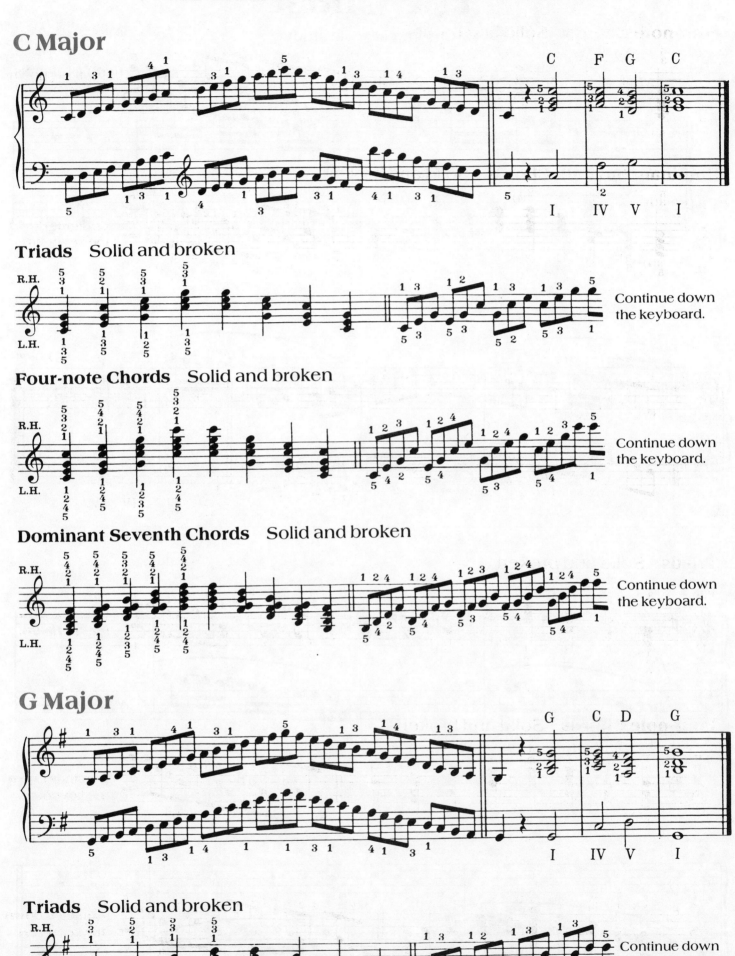

Triads   Solid and broken

Continue down
the keyboard.

Four-note Chords   Solid and broken

Continue down
the keyboard.

Dominant Seventh Chords   Solid and broken

Continue down
the keyboard.

G Major

Triads   Solid and broken

Continue down
the keyboard.

Four-note Chords   Solid and broken

Continue down
the keyboard.

Dominant Seventh Chords   Solid and broken

Continue down
the keyboard.

D Major

Triads   Solid and broken

Continue down
the keyboard.

Four-note Chords   Solid and broken

Continue down
the keyboard.

Continue down
the keyboard.

A Major

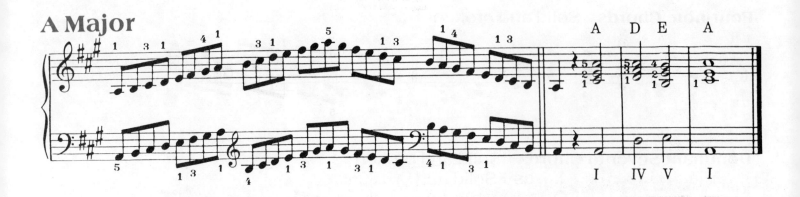

Triads   Solid and broken

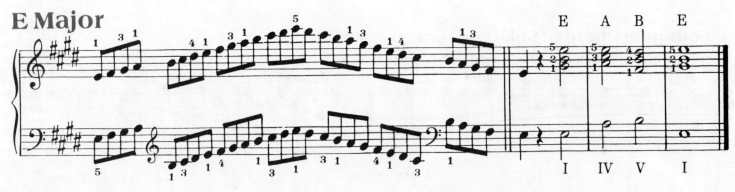

Continue down the keyboard.

Four-note Chords   Solid and broken

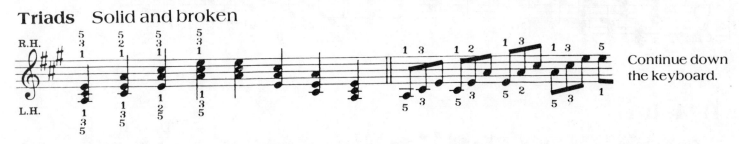

Continue down the keyboard.

Dominant Seventh Chords   Solid and broken

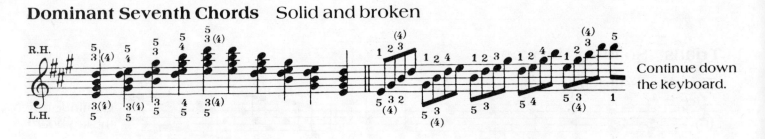

Continue down the keyboard.

E Major

Triads   Solid and broken

Continue down the keyboard.

Four-note Chords   Solid and broken

Continue down the keyboard.

Dominant Seventh Chords   Solid and broken

Continue down the keyboard.

F Major

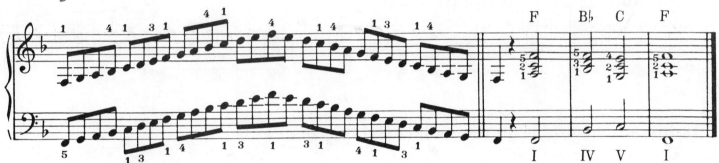

Triads   Solid and broken

Continue down the keyboard.

Four-note Chords   Solid and broken

Continue down the keyboard.

Dominant Seventh Chords   Solid and broken

Continue down the keyboard.

B♭ Major

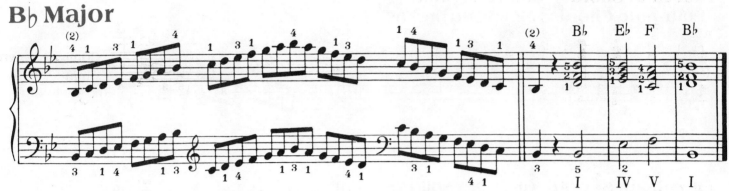

Triads   Solid and broken

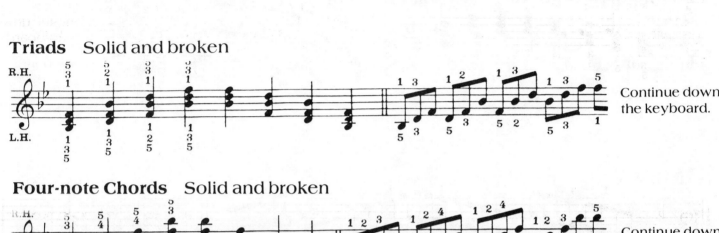

Continue down the keyboard.

Four-note Chords   Solid and broken

Continue down the keyboard.

Dominant Seventh Chords   Solid and broken

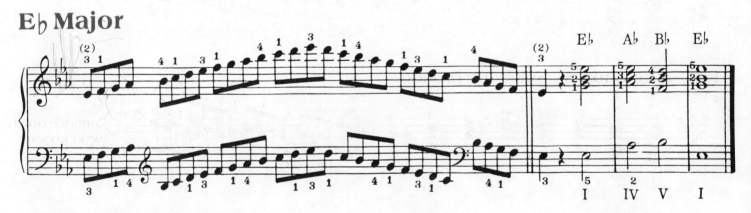

Continue down the keyboard.

E♭ Major

Triads   Solid and broken

Continue down the keyboard.

Four-note Chords   Solid and broken

Continue down
the keyboard.

Continue down
the keyboard.

A♭ Major

Ab   Db   Eb   Ab

I   IV   V   I

Triads   Solid and broken

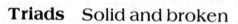

Continue down
the keyboard.

Four-note Chords   Solid and broken

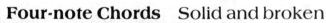

Continue down
the keyboard.

Dominant Seventh Chords   Solid and broken

Continue down
the keyboard.

44

a minor

Am   Dm   E   Am

i   iv   V   i

Triads   Solid and broken

Continue down the keyboard.

Four-note Chords   Solid and broken

Continue down the keyboard.

Diminished Seventh Chords   Solid and broken

(Note: The fingering is the same for each chord; finger 3 or 4 may be used as indicated depending on the size of the hand.)

Continue down the keyboard.

e minor

Em   Am   B   Em

i   iv   V   i

Triads   Solid and broken

Continue down the keyboard.

Four-note Chords   Solid and broken

Continue down
the keyboard.

Diminished Seventh Chords   Solid and broken

(Note: The fingering is the same for each chord; finger 3 or 4 may be used as indicated depending on the size of the hand.)

Continue down
the keyboard.

b minor

Triads   Solid and broken

Continue down
the keyboard.

Four-note Chords   Solid and broken

Continue down
the keyboard.

Diminished Seventh Chords   Solid and broken

(Note: The fingering is the same for each chord; finger 3 or 4 may be used as indicated depending on the size of the hand.)

Continue down
the keyboard.

d minor

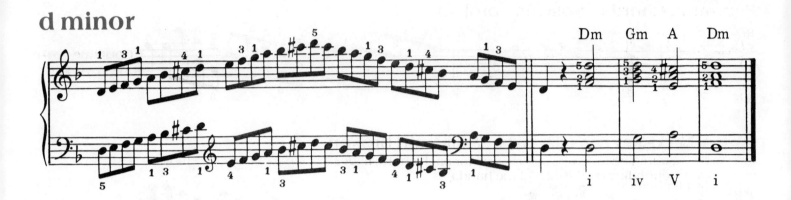

Triads   Solid and broken

Continue down the keyboard.

Four-note Chords   Solid and broken

Continue down the keyboard.

Diminished Seventh Chords   Solid and broken

(Note: The fingering is the same for each chord; finger 3 or 4 may be used as indicated depending on the size of the hand.)

Continue down the keyboard.

g minor

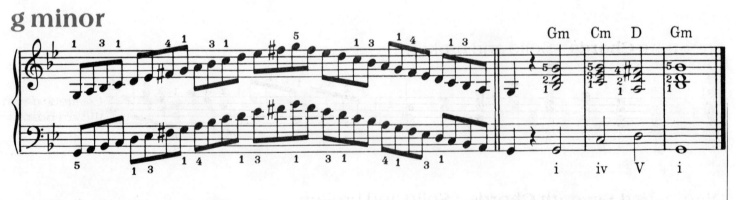

Triads   Solid and broken

Continue down the keyboard.

Four-note Chords   Solid and broken

Continue down the keyboard.

Diminished Seventh Chords   Solid and broken

(Note: The fingering is the same for each chord; finger 3 or 4 may be used as indicated depending on the size of the hand.)

Continue down the keyboard.

c minor

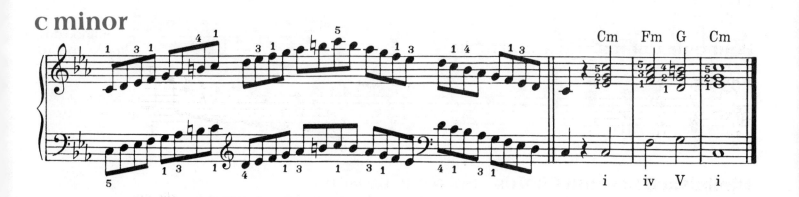

Cm   Fm   G   Cm

i   iv   V   i

Triads   Solid and broken

Continue down the keyboard.

Four-note Chords   Solid and broken

Continue down the keyboard.

Diminished Seventh Chords   Solid and broken

(Note: The fingering is the same for each chord; finger 3 or 4 may be used as indicated depending on the size of the hand.)

Continue down the keyboard.

f minor

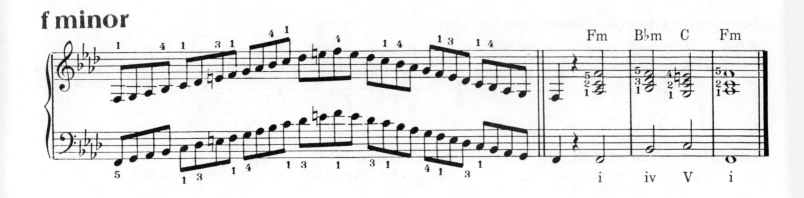

Triads   Solid and broken

Continue down the keyboard.

Four-note Chords   Solid and broken

Continue down the keyboard.

Diminished Seventh Chords   Solid and broken

(Note: The fingering is the same for each chord; finger 3 or 4 may be used as indicated depending on the size of the hand.)

Continue down the keyboard.